Also by Sally Cook, with illustrations by Ross MacDonald

How to Speak Baseball:
An Illustrated Guide to Ballpark Banter

How to Speak Golf:
An Illustrated Guide to Links Lingo

How to Speak Football:
From Ankle Breaker to Zebra:
An Illustrated Guide to Gridiron Gab

In memory of
Cindy and Charlie Crockett

Special thanks to
Max Schwenk and Dugan Zier

HOW *to* SPEAK

SOCCER

Sally Cook

SALLY COOK and **ROSS MACDONALD**

From Assist to Woodwork:
An Illustrated Guide to
Pitch-Perfect Jargon

FLATIRON
BOOKS

HOW TO SPEAK SOCCER. Copyright © 2017 by Sally Cook and Ross MacDonald. Illustrations copyright © 2017 by Ross MacDonald. All rights reserved. Printed in the United States of America. For information, address Flatiron Books, 175 Fifth Avenue, New York, N.Y. 10010.

www.flatironbooks.com

Designed by Mike Gmitter

The Library of Congress Cataloging-in-Publication Data is available upon request.

ISBN 978-1-250-07201-6 (paper over board)
ISBN 978-1-250-07202-3 (e-book)

Our books may be purchased in bulk for promotional, educational, or business use. Please contact your local bookseller or the Macmillan Corporate and Premium Sales Department at 1-800-221-7945, extension 5442, or by e-mail at MacmillanSpecialMarkets@macmillan.com.

First Edition: April 2017

10 9 8 7 6 5 4 3 2 1

INTRODUCTION

Soccer has been a favorite sport all over the world for many years, and its popularity in America has been rapidly growing for decades. For soccer, as with any sport, getting acquainted with the lingo greatly increases the enjoyment of the game.

For example, you may be confused when you hear fans go on and on about "cards." Are they talking poker or soccer? How about when a reporter refers to "group of death," "striker," "booking," or "sudden death"? You might possibly think you're listening to a homicide investigation. When an announcer speaks of a "nutmeg" or a "banana kick," is he offering up some ingredients for dessert? Nope, the announcers, reporters, and fans are most likely just speaking a little soccer.

In this book we've pulled together the most commonly used vernacular and paired some of these terms with zany illustrations that are as intriguing as the language. We've also included various players' nicknames and teams' nicknames. Here you'll find amusing stories plus some history of the sport. We hope that after reading *How to Speak Soccer*, you'll be able to converse with your fellow soccer devotees in no time.

ADDED TIME

ADDED TIME

Minutes tacked on before halftime or at the end of the game, at the referee's discretion, due to excessive flopping, fouling, or injuries during the course of play, which causes play to stop although the clock does not. Added time makes up for the time that is lost while the play was stopped. It is unavoidable, which explains why you will usually see play continue after the clock has reached ninety minutes. Also called stoppage time or injury time.

AGGREGATE

The combined score of two games. Many of soccer's most important club competitions are played on a knockout basis or in an elimination tournament. To decide which teams will play against each other, a draw is conducted. The two clubs drawn as a pair play each other twice, a home and an away game. The winner is then decided by simply adding together the scores from the two games. That is the aggregate score. For example, if the score in one Manchester United vs. Arsenal game was Manchester 2, Arsenal 1, and the second game was Manchester

5, Arsenal 0, the aggregate score would be Manchester 7, Arsenal 1.

If the aggregate score is tied, then the winner is the club that scored more goals on its opponent's field, usually referred to as "the aggregate away-goals rule." If the score is still tied under the away-goals rule, then thirty minutes of overtime are played (usually not sudden death). If that doesn't produce a result, then a penalty shoot-out is used to decide the tie.

AROUND THE WORLD
A freestyle juggling trick. When a player kicks the ball in the air and then swings his leg in a circular motion before kicking it again while in midair.

ASSIST
A pass that leads to a goal scored.

ATTACKING THIRD
The third portion of the field that contains the other team's goal. The offensive team takes greater risks in this zone. Also called defensive third.

AROUND THE WORLD

CORNERKICKS: HAT TRICKS

Many players have scored hat tricks (three goals in the same match) during their lifetime. Yet few have the claim to fame that West Ham and England defender Alvin Martin has regarding hat tricks.

In April 1986 during West Ham's 8–1 home win against Newcastle United, Martin scored three goals against three different goalkeepers, making him the only player to score a hat trick in such a manner. The defender netted his first goal against Newcastle goalkeeper Martin Thomas, who was then replaced by Chris Hedworth because of an injury. Martin then scored against Hedworth, who

was then replaced by Peter Beardsley toward the end of the match, and whom Martin again promptly scored against.

BALL WATCHING

AWAY

A command shouted to a defender, telling him to kick the ball away from his goal.

B TEAM

The reserve team of a club or national team. Usually consists of a combination of up-and-coming youth players as well as first-team squad players.

BACK DOOR

The goal post farthest from the ball. If the ball is on the right side of the goal, the back door is on the left and vice versa.

BACK HEEL

Using the back of the heel to kick the ball.

BALL

(verb) To play hard or well. "You gotta ball."

BALL WATCHING

When a player focuses too much on the ball instead of what is happening on the field or the movement of the other players.

BALLON D'OR

An annual award given by FIFA (Fédération Internationale de Football Association or, in English, International Federation of Association Football) to the player considered to have performed the best in the previous calendar year. The winner is chosen based on the votes from national team coaches and captains, as well as journalists from around the world.

BANANA KICK

Unique kick causing the ball to take a curved path. Also known as an inswinger if it curves in and an outswinger if it curves out. This term is used frequently on corner kicks, which must curve into or away from the goal, and which curve around defenders or around a wall on free kicks.

BEND

A kick that curves in midair.

BETWEEN THE STICKS

The space between the two goalposts.

BICYCLE KICK

When a player jumps up into the air making a shearing movement with his legs (similar to the motion of riding a bicycle) in order to kick the ball. This is one of soccer's most celebrated skills and it can be used defensively to clear the ball away from the goalmouth or offensively to strike at the goal in an attempt to score. Also called *chilena* (in Spanish-speaking countries), overhead kick, or scissors kick.

BOOTS

Cleats or soccer shoes.

BOTTLER

A British colloquialism for a player who initially plays well but then makes a whopping error or lets his team down in a critical situation. The player might lose his temper and get removed from the game, miss a penalty, or miss an easy chance. Entire soccer teams can be referred to as bottlers if they start out strong and then falter terribly toward the end of the season.

CORNERKICKS: WHAT'S IN A NAME? ASSOCIATION FOOTBALL VS. SOCCER

A BRIEF HISTORY OF SOCCER

Various forms of soccer have been played in ancient cultures going back as far as 200 BC in China. But modern soccer most likely evolved from Celtic ball games played in the British Isles during medieval times. Curiously, soccer was thought to incite sin and violence, and a number of kings banned the game.

The modern version of soccer or association football as we know it developed around the mid-1800s in England and Scotland. In 1863, when rules were codified, the beginning of modern soccer began.

Traditional football clubs traveled across the ocean in the mid-nineteenth century and by the 1880s, Canadian and American teams started playing each other in informal matches. "Football clubs" could be found in most of Europe by the early 1900s.

Soon Canada dropped its interest in football to pursue the weather-appropriate sport of ice hockey. But by the early twentieth century a new sport was taking over in the United States: gridiron football, or what the rest of the world now calls American football.

At the same time, the term soccer was starting to catch on. Dated to the late 1800s, the word *socca* was initially formed as an abbreviated version of association football, often used to differentiate the game from rugby football. This shortened slang version evolved in the US from socca to socker and finally soccer.

The US is not completely alone in their preference for soccer. Some sports fans in the British Isles refer to rugby as football, and use soccer the same as Americans do. Soccer is also used in South Africa, Canada, and Australia.

CAPTAIN

BOX-TO-BOX MIDFIELDER

A midfielder who has the stamina to run back and forth between his own and the opposing penalty box, as well as the versatility to play effectively on both offense and defense.

BRACE

When a player scores two goals in a game.

CAP

Symbolic expression for a player's appearance in a game at international level. Before FIFA required teams to wear matching shirts, they wore matching caps. Each time a player appeared in a game for his country, he received a cap. Once teams starting wearing uniforms, they still called the honor of playing in an international match "earning a cap."

CAPTAIN

The leader of the team. He wears the captain's armband so the referee can identify him. The captain is usually selected by the manager, but he can also be chosen by his teammates. Often it is one of the older or more experienced members of the squad, a player that can heavily influence a game, or, as in other sports, the best player on the team. On disciplined teams, the referee communicates mostly with the captains and less with the individual players. The official role of the captain under the Laws of the Game is to participate in the coin toss prior to kickoff (for choice of ends and to determine who kicks off first) and prior to a penalty shootout. Captains have no special power under the Laws to challenge a referee's call during the game. But, referees will sometimes talk to the captain about the team's general behavior if he finds it problematic. Also called skipper.

CHAMPIONS LEAGUE

An annual tournament that includes Europe's best club teams.

CHANNELS

Certain areas of the field, created by the space between players and/or groups of players. There are two types of channels: vertical (between full backs and their closest center back) and horizontal (between defense, midfield, and attack).

CHECK

When a player makes himself available for a pass. Also called show.

CHEEKY

When a player executes a risky or creative move that pays off.

CLEAN SHEET

When a goalkeeper or team doesn't allow any goals to be scored for the entire game. This term dates back to the 1930s, when journalists used sheets of paper to record stats for either team. If one team didn't allow a goal, their sheet remained clean. Also called a shutout.

CLEAR OR CLEARANCE

A situation where a defender is under pressure and kicks the ball aimlessly upfield or out of play. During a clear, the player is only thinking about distance, not placement.

CORNERKICKS: WHERE IN THE FOG WERE THEY?

In 1945 Arsenal and Dynamo Moscow played a friendly match against each other at White Hart Lane in London. As a thick pea-soup fog rolled in, the referee continued the match despite the fog and the anxious requests from players to end the game.

As the weather worsened neither team was able to make headway because of the lack of visibility, and everybody ended up taking advantage of the poor situation. Fans said that Moscow at one

point had fifteen players on the field since they had continued to make substitutions without first removing players.

Arsenal reportedly had a player who had been withdrawn from the game sneak back onto the field and continue to play. But the most extraordinary event of the game occurred when the Arsenal goalkeeper dove for a ball, but due to the fog, miscalculated and hit the goalpost instead, knocking himself out. After a few minutes he recovered, but wasn't able to continue. A spectator ended up taking his position and the match continued. The final score was a 4–3 loss for Arsenal, which almost seemed irrelevant after such antics on the pitch.

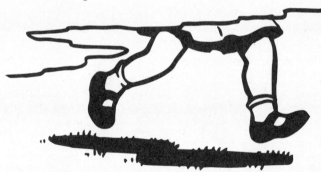

CLIP

When the defender slightly knocks the attacker's heels to take him down.

CLOSE DOWN

When a player runs to close down an attacker's space to maneuver or pass. The attackers are slowed down by this maneuver and, most important, their space to operate is restricted.

CORNER KICK

When a play restarts with a kick taken from one of the two corners in the offensive third of the field. This is a prime goal-scoring opportunity, especially by teams that are adept at heading the ball.

COUNTER (ATTACK)

When an offensive team makes a poor turnover and the opposing team retaliates quickly, creating an advantage in the amount of players on the attack.

COVER THE POST

When a defender stands just inside a goalpost to

assist the goalkeeper in covering the goal. This usually happens on corner kicks.

CLOSE DOWN

CROSS

CROSS

A medium-to long-range pass from a wide area of the field toward the middle of the field near the opponent's goal. The intention is to directly bring the ball into the box from an angle, allowing the attacking forwards to more easily aim for a goal with their head or feet. Crosses are for the most part airborne (floated) to clear nearby defenders, but can also be hit with force along the ground (drilled). A quick and effective move.

CRUYFF

One of the most effective ploys used to lose a defender on the field. A player swings his leg toward the ball (suggesting that he is shooting) but then uses the inside of his kicking foot to drag the ball back behind his planted leg and into the open space opposite the direction where he would have kicked it. This move is named after Johan Cruyff, a former professional soccer player and manager from Holland who is considered one of the greatest players in history. This move was first executed by Cruyff in the 1974 FIFA World Cup when Holland faced off against Sweden, and he outwitted Swedish defender Jan Olsson. The

Cruyff remains one of the most commonly used dribbling tricks in the game and has been copied by players around the world.

DAISY CUTTER

A type of low, hard kick that either stays completely on the ground or hovers just above it. Hence, it trims daisies.

DEAD BALL

When the ball is not in motion. This happens whenever a foul is committed. A free kick is granted to the team against which the foul was made, and there must be a minimum distance of five yards between the ball and the players. Corner kicks as well as goal kicks are considered dead-ball situations. The possibility of scoring a goal increases as the distance between the goal and the ball decreases in a dead-ball situation.

DECOY RUN

A movement made by a player to draw attention away from an attacking teammate. Also called creating space and dummy run.

DEFENDER

An outfield player whose main role is to prevent the opposing team from scoring goals.

DERBY

A rivalry match between teams from the same city, town, or region. Pronounced "darby."

DID UP

When an attacker makes a move around a defender, leaving him behind. Also known as skinned or cut up.

DINKED IT OVER THE KEEPER

When a player deftly lifts the ball over a goalkeeper's head, usually because the goalkeeper is too far out of the penalty box. This is extremely difficult to do, but if executed it's almost impossible for the goalie to recover.

DISPOSSESS

Taking the ball away from an opposing player.

CORNERKICKS: MEN'S TEAM NAMES

ARGENTINA: La Albiceleste means "the white and sky blue" and refers to Argentina's famous striped uniforms.

BRAZIL: Seleção or "the selection" which is what Brazilians call every soccer team. Also known as Little Canary because of their bright yellow shirts.

ENGLAND: The Three Lions refers to the country's history, going back to Richard the Lionheart, king of England from 1189 to 1199. The three lions that appear on the national team's crest also appear on the Royal Arms of England.

FRANCE: Les Bleus or "the blues" which is the name associated with most French sports teams.

ITALY: Azzurri or "the blues," the color of the House of Savoy which unified Italy in 1861.

GERMANY: Die Mannschaft means "the team" in German.

SPAIN: La Furia Roja. During the 1920 Summer Olympics in Antwerp, Spain won a silver medal, popularizing the tiki-taka style of playing, focusing on flair, creativity, and touch. Spain is also known for its direct aggressive and spirited style of play, thus the *furia* or fury. The team also goes by its primary uniform color—La Roja.

UNITED STATES: The Yanks, shortened from Yankees, The Stars and Stripes, and Team USA.

URUGUAY: La Celeste means "the blue sky," referencing the team's sky-blue uniforms.

CORNERKICKS: HOAXSTER EXTRAORDINAIRE

Here's a player most fans have never heard of: Senagalese striker Ali Dia. After struggling in the lower leagues of French football and later failing trials in England, Dia moved to Southampton in 1996. The then-30-year-old devised a plan to play for a Premiership club. He had his agent call Southampton manager Graeme Souness, professing to be George Weah—then world footballer of the year. "Weah" alleged he was the cousin of Dia and proposed that Souness sign him.

Souness was tricked into giving Dia a 30 day contract. Dia played just one game for Southampton, against Leeds United on November 23, 1996. He came on as a substitute for Matthew Le Tissier after 32 minutes but was later substituted himself by Ken Monkou in the 85th minute. After Leeds won the match 2–0, Le Tissier was quoted as saying: "He ran around the pitch like Bambi on ice; it was very embarrassing to watch."

Dia was released by Southampton two weeks into his contract and was never seen on the pitch again.

DIRECT FREE KICK

This is awarded to the opposing team if a player commits any of these seven infringements in a way that the referee considers to be reckless or using excessive force:

• Charges an opponent
• Strikes or attempts to strike an opponent
• Pushes an opponent
• Tackles an opponent
• Kicks or attempts to kick an opponent
• Trips or attempts to trip an opponent
• Jumps at an opponent.

Also awarded to the opposing team if a player commits any of the following:

• Spits at an opponent
• Holds an opponent
• Handles the ball deliberately with his hands (except for the goalkeeper within his own penalty area)

A direct free kick is taken from where the trespass happened. The ball must be motionless when the kick is taken and the kicker is not allowed to touch the ball again until it has touched another player.

A goal is awarded if a direct kick is booted into the opponent's goal. If, for some reason, a direct kick is kicked into a player's team's own goal, a corner kick is then given to the opposing team.

DIRECT PLAY

Playing the ball directly up to the forwards, often bypassing the midfield. The emphasis is getting the ball up the field as quickly as possible, often with little regard for retaining possession. The belief is that if the ball is closer to the goal there is a better chance of scoring, so they try to get it there as quickly as possible. Teams who are considered underdogs may take this approach because they do not have confidence in the quality of their players to be able to pass and be patient with the ball. Also known as boot and chase. Antonym to **tiki-taka**.

DIVING

When a player falls to the ground pretending that he has been injured as if a foul has been committed. In many parts of the world divers are looked down upon and usually are given a card if it is obvious that they are faking. They can even be fined by FIFA for this action. Also known as flopping.

DIVING

DIVING HEADER

When a player dives horizontally to head a ball at knee height.

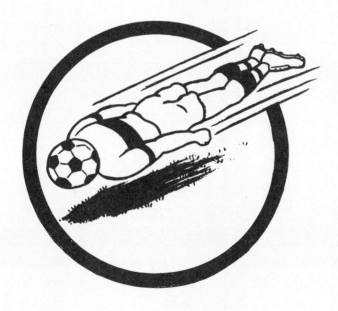

DIVING HEADER

CORNERKICKS: NOT JUST A FRIENDLY GAME OF CARDS

Yellow and red cards are used as a way to discipline players for misconduct during the game. A yellow card is used to caution players, while a red card results in the player's dismissal from the field of play. Thus, yellow cards are used to

punish milder forms of misconduct, while red cards are used for more serious transgressions. A player receives a yellow card for committing any of the following: unsportsmanlike behavior, showing disagreement by word or action, willfully infringing the Laws of the Game, delaying the restart of play, failing to respect the required distance when play is restarted with various kicks, or deliberately entering or leaving the field without the referee's permission. Red cards are issued if a player has already received two yellow cards in the same match or if a player is guilty of serious foul play or violent conduct; uses insulting language or gestures; spits on an opponent or other person; denies the opposing team a goal or obvious goal-scoring chance by handling the ball with his hands; or denies an obvious scoring opportunity to an opponent moving toward the player's goal by an offense punishable by a free kick or penalty kick.

The referee holds the card above his or her head while looking or pointing toward the player that has committed the offense and then records the player's details in a small notebook. A caution is known as a **booking.**

DRIBBLE

A move where a player twists and runs with the ball at his feet.

DUMMY

A tactic used by a player to trick an opponent. He fakes passing the ball but actually keeps possession of it, sometimes dodging in one direction but then taking the ball in another. This move freezes the defense and usually allows the player's teammate more time to make a smarter move. Dummy also means when a player fakes a move in a certain direction or runs to a particular location on the field for the purpose of drawing defenders out of position. Also known as a fake.

EARLY CROSS

Passing the ball into the opposition's box before expected, catching rivals off guard.

EL CLÁSICO

Any match between fierce rivals Real Madrid and Barcelona. Barcelona represents the Catalan people while Read Madrid is linked to Spanish nationalism and the royal family of Spain. Initially it referred only to those competitions held in the Spanish championship, but now the term's usage has been more encompassing, and tends to include every match between the two clubs. Other than the UEFA (Union of European Football Associations) Champions League Final, it is one of the most well-known games in the world and is among the most-viewed annual sporting events.

END LINE
The sideline at each end of the field that runs from one corner flag across the goal mouth to the other corner flag. Also referred to as the byline.

EQUALIZER
A goal that evens the score.

EXTRA TIME
An additional period of play, which usually consists of two halves of fifteen minutes, and is used to determine the winner in some tied cup matches.

CORNERKICKS: MOST UNUSUAL GAME

Soccer games are sometimes played between countries that aren't exactly friendly, but perhaps one of the most unusual games took place between two countries that were at war. On Christmas Day, 1914, British and German troops called an informal truce and jointly observed holiday festivities, including a soccer game. Recollections are hazy but some remember that the British won the game 3–2...and later the war.

FALSE NINE

Similar to an attacking midfielder, this player makes creative forward passes. The number 9 is typically worn by a traditional striker/forward. This player is called a false nine because he is not a striker by trade, but rather a midfielder with exceptionally good technical ability who also scores occasionally. Generally he is there to either crowd the midfield and/or help the team play a more possession-based formation. The number 9 jersey is worn by players deadly anywhere near the penalty area, pure strikers. They are traditionally brilliant finishers. Ronaldo de Lima, Romário, Gabriel Batistuta, Marco van Basten, Samuel Eto'o, and Alan Shearer are some of the greats who wore the number 9. The assignment of jersey numbers by position is a tradition and not a rule. Teams are free to assign numbers to their players as they wish.

FAR POST

The goalpost farthest away from where the ball is.

FEED IT TO THE BIG MAN

Sending the ball to a physically large striker.

FEED IT TO THE BIG MAN

CORNERKICKS: HISTORY OF THE BALL, PART 1

Inflated pig bladders were used as balls during medieval times. However, because of their lack of shape retention and ease of rupture, pig bladders started to be covered in leather. Soccer balls became rounder and lasted longer with the leather covers.

It wasn't until the nineteenth century that a soccer ball was developed that was similar to today's ball.

In the mid-1800s Charles Goodyear patented vulcanized rubber and built the first vulcanized soccer balls. Vulcanization gave the ball its strength, elasticity, and resistance to solvents and moderate heat and cold, and increased the bounce, making the ball easier to kick. Before this, balls were whatever the size and shape of the pig's bladder. The uneven shape of the ball, because of the irregularity of the bladder, caused it to have an erratic flight pattern.

By 1863, the newly formed English Football Association, soccer's governing body, met to establish rules of the game. These rules contained no reference to the dimensions of the ball. But in 1872, the association met again and rewrote the rules. The ball's dimensions were decided upon, and according to the English Football Association: "The ball must be spherical with a circumference of 27 to 28 inches with a weight at the start of the game of 13–15 ounces." Today these rules are enforced by FIFA and only changed again in 1937 when the weight of the ball increased to 14–16 ounces. The 1953 edition of the English Encyclopedia of Football states:

"According to the Laws of Football, the ball must be spherical with an outer casing of leather or other approved materials. The circumference shall not be more than 28 inches, nor less than 27 inches, while the weight at the start of the game must not be more than 16 oz., nor less than 14 oz." These ball specifications have remained the same since then; only the construction materials and designs have changed.

FIRST TOUCH

FEINT

When a particular player deceives the opposition into believing he is going to pass, shoot, move in a certain direction, or receive the ball, but instead does something entirely different, thus gaining an advantage.

FIFTY-FIFTY BALL

A loose ball or a badly placed pass that puts the ball as close to a player of one team as it does to a player of the opposing team, giving both an equal chance of controlling it.

FINISH

To score a goal by placing the ball in the back of the opponent's net.

FIRST TOUCH

When a player has the ability to bring the ball entirely under control immediately upon receiving it. The player places his body or feet in such a way that he can quickly gain authority over the ball, and from there he can do whatever he pleases with it: stop it, continue its momentum, or move it from danger.

FIST

When goalkeepers punch a high-flying ball that is difficult to control. Also called boxing.

FIXTURE

A scheduled match.

FLANK

The left- or right-most side of the field.

FLICK

A light touch by an outfield player using his head or foot that quickly and effectively diverts the ball to a teammate. For a goalkeeper, a flick is any sudden movement of the hand that deflects a shot or header bound for the goal.

FLIGHTED BALL

A pass that is lofted through the air.

FOOTBALLER

Another term for soccer player, originating in countries where soccer is referred to as football.

FOOTY

A colloquial name for football (soccer) in Europe.

FORMATION

The selection and strategic alignment of players, which a team can often stay in quite rigidly. Other times a formation can be more fluid, depending on the manager/coach.

FORWARD

The main job of this player is to score goals or to set them up for teammates. A center forward, also called a striker, should be a team's leading goal scorer. He is known as the most dangerous player in the attacking third of the field.

FOUL

An unfair act by a player, which leads to stoppage of the game. If the referee thinks an action is breaking the game's rules he calls a foul to protect the players and keep the game fair. Fouls are penalized by the award of a free kick (direct or indirect depending on the transgression) to the offended team, or a penalty kick to the offending team. Aggressive physical play and inappropriate handling of the ball constitute most fouls. Furthermore, a foul can only be committed by a player (not a substitute) on the field while the ball is in play. Where applicable, fouls are limited to acts committed against an opponent (for example, a player striking the referee or a teammate is not a foul, but is misconduct).

FOX IN THE BOX

A type of striker, mostly known for his outstanding ability to score and his deft movements inside the penalty area. Also known as a goal poacher.

FROG

A dribbling technique where the player jumps with the ball clamped between his feet.

FULLBACK

A defensive player who is situated to the right or left of the team's center back.

GAFFER

The head coach or manager. This term is most often used in Europe.

GOAL BOX

An area of eighteen square yards in which the goalkeeper, but no field player, can handle the ball. Its primary purpose is to mark out the goalkeeper's area of influence on the field. Also called the penalty box.

GOAL DIFFERENTIAL

The number of goals a team has scored minus the number they have allowed.

GOAL KICK

A ball that is put back into play by the goalkeeper without challenge by the opposing team. It is required that a goal kick is made from the ground within the goal box. During a goal kick the opponents must be behind the eighteen-yard penalty area and the ball must leave the box before any other player can touch it.

CORNERKICKS: WHO INVENTED RED AND YELLOW CARDS?

Ken Aston (1915–2001), an English teacher, soldier, and one of soccer's toughest and most esteemed referees, was responsible for introducing red and yellow cards, which were first used in the 1970 World Cup. In 1966, Aston, a Brit, was officiating a game and contemplating some controversial decisions that had been made in a recent match between England and Argentina. At one point, an Argentinian player was trying to communicate with a German referee, and his pleas, incoherent to the ref, got him expelled for

"violence of the tongue." The Argentinian player wouldn't leave the field until Aston mediated. Then, a furious Argentinian team supposedly tried to break into the English locker room after losing the heated match. Driving home after the game, Aston pulled up to a stoplight. In a July 8, 2014, article in *Smithsonian* magazine by Jimmy Stamp, Aston is quoted as saying, "As I drove down Kensington High Street, the traffic light turned red. I thought, 'Yellow, take it easy; red, stop, you're off.' Thus the system of red and yellow cards was born. Aston's inspiration that evening is now used to indicate warnings and penalties in more than a dozen other games, including fencing, field hockey, volleyball, and water polo.

GOAL-LINE TECHNOLOGY

This technology instantly determines whether or not the entirety of a ball has crossed between the goalposts and underneath the crossbar. This method assists the referee in deciding whether to award a goal or not. It doesn't replace the role of the officials, but rather supports them in their decision-making. It was first used at the 2014 FIFA World Cup in Brazil.

GOALKEEPER

The goalkeeper is the only one of the eleven players on the field who is allowed to use his hands during play and guards their team's goal. The use of his hands is limited to the rectangular penalty area extending eighteen yards from each side of the goal.

GIVE-AND-GO

The most fundamental passing combination. It involves two teammates and two passes to get around, or "beat," a single defender. The player with the ball dribbles toward the defender straight on, but then passes to a teammate who has come toward the defender at a right angle; the first player then runs around the defender and receives a return pass from his teammate. Also known as wall pass, one-two, or 2 v 1. This passing combination is similar to ones used in basketball, ice hockey, field hockey, and lacrosse.

GOAL-LINE TECHNOLOGY

GOLDEN GOAL

An overtime session where the team to score the first goal wins. Also called sudden death.

GROUP OF DEATH

First coined from the Spanish *grupo de la muerte* by a Mexican journalist for Group 3 of the 1970 World Cup. Refers to the group containing the strongest teams or the strongest team in a tournament. The group phase is part of many tournaments. Every team in the group (typically four) will play each other. The team with the most points after the group phase progresses into the knockout stage of the tournament. In that phase, the team is either knocked out immediately upon losing (as in the World Cup) or it advances or drops out based on the aggregate score (as in the Champions League and Europa League). All tournament finals end in a single elimination game. In other words, no tournaments are decided in the championship game with an aggregate score.

HACK
A purposeful foul.

HALF VOLLEY
Kicking the ball while it is in the air but after it has already bounced one or more times. Often easier to execute than a full volley (no bounce).

HANDBALL
The act of touching the ball with the hand or arm (doesn't include shoulder). When a non-goalkeeper touches the ball inside the penalty box, it may result in a penalty kick depending on whether he appeared to do it intentionally or not. Outside the box, the result may be a free kick. This is probably the most contentious call in soccer because usually the intent determines the outcome, but intent may be difficult to determine.

Handballs do not apply to the goalkeeper when inside his own penalty area.

CORNERKICKS: HISTORY OF THE BALL: PART 2

By the 1900s the vulcanized "bladders" used for soccer balls were created from inner tubes with stronger rubber that could endure heavier pressure. Most balls had a tanned leather cover with eighteen sections stitched together in six panels of three strips each. These bounced more easily than the others. Each section was sewn together by hand with five-ply hemp and a small lace-up slit on one side. All of the stitching was done with the ball cover inside out. Once finished, the cover was inverted with the stitching on the inside. The small slit allowed for an inflated rubber bladder to be inserted into it.

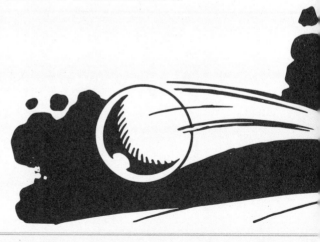

The balls had to be re-inflated frequently and while they were perfect for bouncing and kicking, heading them (hitting them with the player's head) was frequently painful, especially in the area of the ball that contained the heavy leather laces. Moreover, the leather in the ball often absorbed water from rain, causing a significant increase in weight, which often resulted in head or neck injuries. Over the first five World Cups, the ball changed so that the leather became thinner and less hard, and the sewing pattern moved toward a standard of sorts: strips of leather arranged at ninety-degree angles.

For the 1940 World Cup, architect, mathematician, and designer of the geodesic dome, Buckminster Fuller, created a ball consisting of twelve pentagons and twenty hexagons that was closer to a true sphere. In the 1950s synthetic paints were used to waterproof leather balls. In 1951 white soccer balls were manufactured to improve ball visibility for players and spectators. Orange soccer balls were used in snowy venues.

It wasn't until 1970 that Adidas introduced

today's black-and-white ball. Made specifically for the 1970 World Cup, it has thirty-two panels that were alternately painted in black and white (twenty panels were in white and twelve in black). Named the Telstar, after the space satellite that it resembles, its pattern made the ball more visible on black-and-white television. This ball was once again used in the 1974 World Cup and it was there that FIFA announced it as the official soccer ball for the very first time.

Until the 2006 World Cup the thirty-two-panel ball was the standard. Then Adidas introduced a fourteen-paneled ball called the Teamgeist (German for team spirit). Fewer panels made the ball smoother. The panels were bonded together instead of being stitched for a more even surface. For the 2010 World Cup, Adidas presented an eight-panel ball called the Jubalani (a South African word for celebrate) which featured fewer panels and better polyurethane materials which improved the ball's performance and feel.

The current regulation ball has only six large panels and the inside now contains a latex bladder. The ball's panel pairs are stitched along the edge, either manually or with a machine. For a regulation size-five ball, the diameter is about 8.65 inches.

Local suppliers made the earliest balls wherever the game was played. Today it is estimated that forty percent of all soccer balls are manufactured in Pakistan, with other major producers being China and India.

HAT TRICK

Scoring three goals in a single match—a rare occurrence. Also referred to as a treble.

HEADER

Using the head as a means of passing, clearing, or shooting the ball.

HOLDING ROLE OR HOLDING MIDFIELDER

A central midfielder whose main role is to protect the defense.

HOLD UP THE BALL

When a player, usually a forward, receives a long ball (when the ball moves a long distance down the field) from a teammate, and controls and protects it from the opposition with the focus of slowing the play down to allow teammates to join the attack.

HOLDING THE LINE

An imaginary line that the defensive unit makes on the field. The defending team will hold this line and not follow attackers past it. This is a strategy employed on free kicks to try to get the

HAT TRICK

HOLE

opposing attacker called for offsides. The line is often used to reduce the size of the no-man's-land.

HOLE
The space on a field between the midfield and the forwards. In formations where attacking midfielders or deep-lying forwards (a forward who is staying deep into his own team's territory to help link up play with his other teammates) are used, they are said to be "playing in the hole."

HOLLYWOOD BALL
A spectacular-looking long-range pass that ends up being more of a display of technical ability than an effective offensive pass.

HOSPITAL PASS
A slow or misguided pass to a teammate that puts them in danger of getting hurt. Usually this results in the recipient being tackled aggressively or losing the ball easily.

HOWLER
A blatant and possibly amusing error made by

a player or referee during a match. Also when a goalie makes an egregious mistake.

HUG THE POST
A command given to a defender, specifically during corner kicks, to carefully block the area near the post where a goal is likely to be scored.

HUMDINGER
A highly anticipated or exhilarating match.

INTERNATIONAL FOOTBALL ASSOCIATION BOARD
The body that determines the rules of the game for association football or soccer. Also known as IFAB.

INDIRECT FREE KICK
A free kick that is granted to the opposing team if a goalkeeper commits any of these offenses inside his own penalty area:
• Touches the ball with his hands after he has received it directly from a throw-in by a teammate
• Touches the ball with his hands after he has freed it from possession and before it has touched another player

• Touches the ball with his hands after it has been intentionally kicked to him by a teammate

Also awarded to the opposing team if, in the judgment of the referee, a player:
• Hinders the progress of an opponent
• Plays in an unsafe manner
• Prevents the goalkeeper from releasing the ball
• Commits any other transgression for which play is stopped to caution or send off a player

The indirect free kick is taken from the spot where the wrongdoing occurred, and the ball must be stationary before the kick. The kicker is not allowed to touch the ball again until it has touched another player. Only if the ball touches another player before it enters the goal can a goal be scored. If an indirect kick is shot directly into the opponents' goal then a goal kick is taken. Like a direct free kick, if, for some reason, an indirect kick is kicked directly into a player's own goal, a corner kick is awarded to the opposing team.

INSIDE FORWARD
A position employed in a 2-3-5 formation.

The inside forward plays just behind the center forward, similar to the modern attacking midfielder or second striker.

INSTEP DRIVE
A hard and straight shot taken with the instep of the foot.

INTERCEPT
When a player prevents a pass from getting to its intended recipient.

INTERVAL
The fifteen-minute break in between halves. The duration of the game is ninety minutes; each half is forty-five minutes. The players return to the locker room during the interval to rest and confer with coaches.

JOURNEYMAN
When a player has played for many different teams in his career.

KEEPER
The goalkeeper.

KEEPY-UPPIE

Juggling the ball.

KILLER BALL

A pass that reaches a teammate at a flawless angle and opportune time. It permits the player to score a goal easily. Also called killer pass.

KIT

A British term for a soccer uniform.

LAY-OFF

A short backward pass that allows a teammate to join the attacking play effectively. This move is often used to set up a shot on a goal. The implication is that the player receiving the lay-off is facing the opposing goal.

LEATHERED IT

When a player kicks a ball extremely hard.

LEVEL

Tied game.

CORNERKICKS: PLAYER NICKNAMES

The suffix -inho in Portuguese acts as a diminutive meaning "little." It is used as a term of endearment. Most Brazilian players are known by a nickname, not their real names. For instance, the Brazilian star Ronaldo de Assis Moreira is known as "Ronaldinho" which means little Ronaldo, a flattering name for a superb player.

DUNCAN FERGUSON: The Scottish former player was nicknamed "Duncan Disorderly" because of his acerbic, confrontational style.

DAVID BECKHAM: David's wife, Victoria Beckham, or Posh Spice (one of the former Spice Girls), was on a UK chat show when she revealed that her name for the former English soccer player was "Goldenballs." The newspapers ran with it and his nickname stuck.

ZINEDINE YAZID ZIDANE: The former French player was nicknamed "Zizou" when he played for Bordeaux in the 1990s. Zizou comes from the initials of his first and last name. He is called

"Yaz" by his close friends.

FRANZ BECKENBAUER: It is said that the German former player and manager was known as "Der Kaiser" (emperor) because of his elegant style and dominance on the field.

STUART PEARCE: The English player and manager is nicknamed "Psycho" because he sometimes kicked players on the field in the 1980s.

HARRY KEWELL: The Australian soccer coach and former player got the nickname "The Wizard of Oz" because of his many magical moments on the field.

PETER CROUCH: The English striker has several nicknames. The fans and media refer to him as "Crouchy" or "Robo Crouch." In 2006 he adopted a robotic dance whenever he scored a goal. He is also referred to as "Cronchinho," "Mr. Roboto," or "Pantera Rosa" (the Pink Panther) by Spanish commentators.

OLE GUNNAR SOLSKJAER: A Norwegian manager and former player who went by the name of "Baby-Faced Assassin." The British media gave him his nickname because of his youthful looks and deadly finishing.

LIONEL MESSI: The Argentinian player is known as "La Pulga Atomica" or the atomic flea. Diagnosed with a growth-hormone disorder as a child, the Barcelona forward was treated with artificial hormones and developed into a still-small but powerful soccer player. He is also popularly known as just "Leo."

STEVEN GERRARD: He became the captain of the Liverpool team at age twenty-three. He was so successful that he quickly became known as "Mr. Liverpool" or "Captain Fantastic."

HEATHER ANN O'REILLY: The American midfielder has long been known as "HAO" after the initials of her name, pronounced hey-oh. Sometimes "HAO" calls Women's World Cup Champion Kelley O'Hara "KO."

RACHEL BUEHLER: A former American soccer defender, known as "The Buehldozer" or "Dozer" because of her tough playing style.

MANUEL FRANCISCO DOS SANTOS: A former Brazilian player who overcame physical disabilities to become one of the world's greatest soccer players is called "Garrincha," which means wren. He was so small as a child that his sister gave him this nickname, which stuck throughout his life.

LOAN

When a player is allowed to play for another team typically for six to twelve months even though he is owned by one team. Usually this happens because the parent team has an abundance of players in that specific position; the player is normally younger and in need of first team experience.

LONG BALL

A type of pass used to cover a great distance. When used in the right scenario, almost always in the air.

MAGIC COLD SPRAY

A spray used by medics when a player suffers a hit. It is used to numb the area of pain.

MAN BETWEEN THE STICKS

The goalkeeper.

MISSED A SITTER

A flubbed goal or a missed goal-scoring opportunity that even the most jinxed of players could not possibly miss.

MIDFIELDER

The player that plays between the defense and attack. Midfielders are expected to run the most in a game and they are usually the most physically fit players on the field. Midfielders are required to infiltrate deep into enemy territory on an attack and also to make the transition to defense when the opposition keeps possession of the ball.

MLS

Major League Soccer in the U.S. and Canada.

NATIONAL TEAM

An all-star team of players who are citizens of the same country. It is considered a great honor and accomplishment for a player to be selected for their national team. Over two hundred national teams worldwide compete to qualify for the FIFA World Cup.

NEAR POST

The goal post nearest to the ball.

NIL

British term for zero or nothing. "The score was 2–nil."

NO-MAN'S-LAND

The space between the back line and the goalie where it is unclear whose responsibility it is to clear/claim the ball.

NUMBER 10

A midfielder considered to be the primary playmaker and leader on the team. He sometimes actually wears the number 10 and often plays in the hole. Pelé and Diego Maradona (two of the game's greatest) wore the number 10. Also referred to as a *trequartista,* an Italian term.

NUTMEG

When an attacker kicks, rolls, or throws the ball through the defender's legs and receives it on the other side. This move is considered the ultimate triumph over a defender because there is essentially no recovery from it. Also called a meg or tunnel.

OFFSIDES

A player is in the offsides position if he is closer to the goal line than both the ball and the second-to-last defender, but only if he is in the opposition's half of the field. A player is only penalized for being offsides if he is considered to be in active play, interferes with play as part of an attacking move, or has attained any advantage by being in that position.

OFFSIDE TRAP

A play made by the defenders by swiftly moving upfield, away from their goal, causing the attacking team to be offside right as the ball is played by the attackers.

ONION BAG

The goal's netting.

ONE-TOUCH

Shooting or passing an oncoming ball without controlling it first.

ONE V ONE

One player versus one player or one on one. Pronounced one VEE one.

CORNERKICKS: FOOD FOR THOUGHT

The buying and selling of players is typically decided by the price or amount of the transfer fee, often resulting in astounding transactions. Signings are chiefly about adding quality to a team or building a squad. However, here's some food for thought: There are three players who were actually bought or sold for libations or grub.

In 2006 Romanian defender Marius Cioara of second division UT Arad was sold to fourth division side Regal Hornia for about 35 pounds of pork sausage. But, the next day, Cioara retired from soccer, stating he couldn't take any more insulting sausage taunts. Regal Hornia then demanded their stipend back from UT Arad.

Manchester United was interested in buying Stockport County winger Hugh McLenahan in 1927. However, County was in financial straits at the time. United's assistant manager Louis Rocca owned an ice cream business and donated some of his ice cream to a Stockport fundraiser.

Many gallons later United had "scooped" up McLenahan.

Left-back Ernie Blenkinsop, while playing for Cudworth United Methodists of Barnsley, was spotted by the Hull City Tigers in 1921. The Tigers liked what they saw but didn't want to part with a lot of money for the gifted future star. So they settled on a couple of hundred dollars plus a barrel of beer to be shared among Blenkinsop's former teammates.

OWN GOAL

When a player scores in his or her own team's goal, usually by accident. An own goal may result from an attempt at a defensive play that was either unsuccessful or was unexpectedly intercepted by an opposing player. This is considered to be one of the more embarrassing bloopers. Own goals are counted as regular goals.

PANCAKE

When a player is juggling the ball and places his foot flat on the ground and lets the ball hit it, which then results in the ball popping right back up to him.

PANENKA PENALTY

Named after Antonín Panenka, a player who helped his team win the 1976 Euro Championship for Czechoslovakia against West Germany. His penalty is famous because he approached the ball as if he was going to kick it to a corner, but instead chipped it straight down the middle slowly while the goalkeeper dove in the wrong direction and could not recover to get the ball. This move shows both arrogance and confidence and is an

ONE V ONE

example of being cheeky.

PARKING THE BUS
When a team puts all their players behind the ball when defending their goal. A conservative strategy, usually done when one team is an extreme underdog.

PENALTY BOX
The box that extends eighteen yards from the goal, where a penalty kick may be awarded for a foul on the attacking team. If a foul occurs within this area it results in a penalty kick from twelve yards out. The goalkeeper of the team defending this goal can use his hands in this area. Also known as **penalty area.**

PITCH
The field of play. Strangely, there is no precise size for a soccer pitch. The only regulations are that it must be between 110 and 120 yards long and 70 to 80 yards wide. Teams who like to have a lot of possession of the ball (Arsenal and Barcelona for instance) tend to have larger fields.

PLACED (SHOT OR PASS)

A shot or pass that is delicately but intentionally taken, such that its trajectory (slow/fast/low/high) is more important than its power.

PARKING THE BUS

CORNERKICKS: WOMEN'S TEAM NAMES

ENGLAND: Three Lionesses or Lionesses. England's men's team has worn the three lions on their shirts ever since the first international match against Scotland in 1872. The lions come from an old Plantagenet coat of arms. The Plantagenets were kings of medieval England.

GERMANY: Die Nationaleif simply means "the national eleven."

JAPAN: Nadeshiko means "pink flower," symbolizing the ideals of Japanese womanhood. In 2002 the Japanese Football Association held a contest and this nickname was chosen out of 2,700 entries.

NORTH KOREA: Chollima translates as "thousand-mile horse," a Korean mythical horse, and references the players' speed on the field.

USA: USWNT (US Women's National Team). Also called **Stars and Stripes** and **The Yanks,** similar to the U.S. men's teams.

POINTYBALL

POINTYBALL

A term soccer fans use for American football. It refers to the pigskin's pointed ends.

PRESSING/CLOSING DOWN THE OTHER TEAM

This tactic involves closing down the space for the opposition attackers in a coordinated manner to try to force them to lose the ball.

PROMOTION

When a team from a lower division moves up to a higher division as a result of finishing in the top three, usually, of the lower division.

PROFESSIONAL FOUL

When a defender fouls an attacking player in order to prevent him from scoring. The resulting free kick or penalty may be more difficult for the attacking team to score than the original playing position, which is why a defender may have an incentive to strategically foul an attacking player. In 1982 the Football League, soccer's governing body in England, recommended that any transgression that denies the attacking player an obvious scoring opportunity be considered "serious foul play" and the offending player receive a red card, in order to deter offenders. This foul is informally known as DOGSO, an acronym for "denying an obvious goal-scoring opportunity." Also known as a tactical foul.

PUNCH

When a goalie doesn't have enough certainty in his ability to catch a ball from a cross, he instead punches it a good distance away to clear any danger.

PUSH UP

When the back line moves forward to condense the space that the other team has to play in.

RABONA

A type of pass where the kicking leg wraps around the back of the standing leg, making the player's legs effectively crossed. This is also the name of a dance step in the tango which takes its name from the soccer kick.

PUNCH

CORNERKICKS: DOG GONE

During the quarterfinal between England and Brazil at the 1962 World Cup in Chile, a small black dog suddenly entered the field of play. The referee stopped the game but no one could catch the pup. Jimmy Greaves, England's third highest goal scorer of all time, got down on his hands and knees and called the canine over to him. As the fans cheered he picked up the dog and cuddled him. The dog then urinated on his white shirt and unfortunately in those days there was no change of clothes allowed so he had to play in his soiled shirt. One of the Brazilian players, superstar Garrincha, ultimately adopted the dog, which led Greaves to call himself Garrincha's dogcatcher.

RAINBOW KICK

RAINBOW KICK

A trick kick that is done by flicking the ball with the back of the heel and over one's head. It is usually employed to avoid a sliding tackle.

REDIRECT

Touching the ball to change its trajectory; most often this is done intentionally.

RELEGATION

The reverse of **promotion**. Usually the bottom three teams in a league move down a division. In many leagues the amount of money needed to run a club in different divisions is so large that moving up or down a division can profoundly affect the club negatively or positively. Similar to the problems that can arise within cities that hold the Olympics, a promoted team can deal with a long-term issue like a huge influx of cash or publicity. However, if a team is suddenly relegated then they may have to restructure the team's finances so that they are not ruined down the line.

RESERVES

Players who don't make the bench for a game (only eighteen can be on the roster for any given game), so they generally play against the other team's reserves.

RIGHT BACK

A right-sided defender whose job is to attack.

ROCKET

A shot that is struck with immense power.

SEAL DRIBBLE

Juggling the ball with the head while running up the field, imitating a seal. It is difficult to stop someone who is seal dribbling without fouling him.

SENT OFF

A player is sent off after receiving a red card and cannot return to the field. His team must then play with one less player than their opponents for the remainder of the game.

SET PIECE

A free kick, corner kick, or throw-in to restart the game using a choreographed play.

SHIELD

When players use their bodies to protect the ball from the defender.

ROCKET

CORNERKICKS: WOMEN'S WORLD CUP

Held sixty-one years after the first FIFA World Cup, the FIFA Women's World Cup was the inaugural world championship game for the women's national association football teams. It took place in Guangdong, China, in 1991.

Michelle Akers scored ten goals, including five in one game, becoming the lead scorer. She led the US women's team to the first women's world championship, defeating Norway 2–1. Regulation time for matches for the first WWC was eighty minutes—two periods of forty minutes. But the women proved that they had as much endurance as male soccer players, so the competition regulations for the second tournament in 1995 were changed to ninety minutes—two periods of forty-five minutes each, the same as the men's competition.

SHOT INTO THE SIDE NETTING

Placed into the side netting of the goal. A shot aimed there is more likely to go in because the goalkeeper stands in the center. Shot into the wrong side of the side netting is when the ball goes out of play because it hits the outside of the goal.

SIDE VOLLEY

Using a scissoring motion, similar to a bicycle kick, but doing it while standing on the ground.

SIX-POINTER

Describes a game between two teams with similar positions in leagues that employ a "three-points-for-the-win" system. It's called a six-pointer because three points are at play for each team.

If one team wins, three points are gained by that team and the other team remains at zero.

SKIED A SHOT

When the shooter misses the net by a great distance over the crossbar.

SLIDE ACROSS

When the defense moves as a unit from one side of the field to the other, making it harder for the attacking team to score.

SNAKE

An incredibly difficult move performed by pushing the ball with the outside of your foot, then quickly transferring the ball to one's big toe area creating a whiplash, hence the name. The Brazilian player Ronaldinho has successfully performed it more than anyone else. Also known as elastico.

SOMBRERO

A trick where a player steps to the side of the ball and flicks his standing foot upward, propelling the ball forward and over his head, around from the sides of his opponents. The trajectory of the ball gives the move its name. It is usually performed while moving forward with the ball. Also called **rainbow kick** or **reverse flick-over.**

SOPHOMORE SLUMP

When a player struggles and begins to decline after having a good rookie season.

SQUARE PASS

A pass that travels horizontally.

STANDING ROOM

Parts of the stadium where there are no seats and supporters can only stand. These areas are outlawed in most of Europe because of hooliganism during the 1980s.

STEP-OVER

When a player steps around the ball while it is in his possession. When this is done quickly enough it can be hard for a defender to tell whether the player is executing a step-over or actually moving the ball in the direction he is stepping over.

STRIKER

One of the four main positions in soccer. Strikers are the players who are closest to the opponent's goal and whose primary role is to score goals. Often they make creative runs behind the defense and are exceptional finishers. Also known as forward or attacker.

SUBSTITUTE

When one player is taken out and another is put in as a replacement. Three are allowed in a game.

SUBSTITUTE

CORNERKICKS: THE WORLD CUP

Established by FIFA in 1930, the World Cup brings together the world's best men's teams and is also the most-watched sporting event anywhere. The competition has been played every four years since the inaugural tournament, except that it was not held in 1942 and 1946 because of the Second World War. Eight national teams have won the nineteen FIFA World Cup tournaments. Brazil, the one team to have won five times, is the only team to have played in every tournament. The other winners are Italy, with four titles; Germany, with three; Argentina and inaugural winner Uruguay, with two; and England, France, and Spain, with one title each.

TARGET FORWARD OR TARGET MAN

SUPPORTER

A fan.

SWITCH

A long pass or a series of short plays that switch the point of attack from one side of the field to the other.

TARGET FORWARD OR TARGET MAN

A forward who is normally very large and is used to retain possession of the ball while his teammates move up the field so that he can then make a pass. This player is used as an easy transition between offense and defense.

THREE POINTS

A win. "We've got three points."

THROUGH BALL

A ball played either on the ground or in the air, often diagonally, that is sent ahead of an attacking player who then runs on to receive it so the team can take their momentum with the ball. Many assists are a result of through balls.

TIKI-TAKA

A type of play popularized by the Spanish
national team and then-coach Pep Guardiola.
The play consists of fast, short passes, moving
the defense to one side of the field then quickly
moving it back to the other now-vulnerable side.
This is extremely effective play and requires the
highest-quality players to execute it.

TOP FLIGHT

The first division; usually refers to the English
Premier League when discussing British soccer
teams.

TRAP

A first touch on a ball played in the air, where the
ball is brought under control after being received
at a strange angle or high speed. Hence the name
"trap," as if the ball needs to be tamed.

WAGS

A British tabloid abbreviation for wives and
girlfriends of high-profile players. It may also be
used in the singular form to refer to a specific
female partner.

TRAP

CORNERKICKS: NO LAUGHING MATTER

It was a beautiful spring morning in the Danish town of Noerager in April 1960. The match between Noerager and Ebeltoft was just about to end with Noerager leading by one point—4–3. The referee, Henning Erikstrup, glanced at his watch and then proceeded to blow the final whistle. There was just one slight problem: his false teeth fell out of his mouth and landed on the ground. He puffed and puffed on the whistle but no sound came out. Finally Erikstrop knelt to the ground and scrambled to find his dentures while Ebeltoft scored, making the game 4–4. Erikstrop immediately disallowed the goal, arguing that he had actually blown the whistle. He then handed Noerager a 4–3 win. Ebeltoft immediately protested the loss of the match and took the result to what was the equivalent of the Football Association of Denmark. However, their protests were rejected. The final score was Noerager 4, Ebeltoft 3.

WALL

A line of defenders who protect their net during a free kick. The wall must be 10 yards away from where the ball is placed.

WAVE

When fans stand together, yell in succession, and move their arms around a soccer stadium. This movement's effect makes it look like a wave moving throughout the stadium seats. This was originally done by Mexican fans but now is done worldwide.

WOODWORK

The goal frame.

ABOUT THE AUTHORS

SALLY COOK

Sally Cook is the author, with James Charlton, of *How to Speak Baseball* and *Hey Batta Batta Swing! The Wild Old Days of Baseball,* illustrated by Ross MacDonald. She and Ross MacDonald have also coauthored *How to Speak Golf* and *How to Speak Football.* She coauthored, with legendary football coach Gene Stallings, *Another Season: A Coach's Story of Raising an Exceptional Son,* a *New York Times* bestseller.

ROSS MACDONALD

Ross MacDonald's illustrations have appeared in *The New York Times, The New Yorker, Rolling Stone, Harper's, The Atlantic Monthly,* and *Vanity Fair.* He has also written and illustrated several books for children and adults. His most recent is *What Would Jesus Craft?*